For Joel —
with appreciation
and high regard —
— Peter.

D1124726

O WHEEL

O WHEEL

POEMS BY PETER SACKS

THE UNIVERSITY OF GEORGIA PRESS

ATHENS AND LONDON

Published by the University of Georgia Press
Athens, Georgia 30602
© 2000 by Peter Sacks
All rights reserved
Set in eleven on thirteen Aldus by G & S Typesetters
Printed and bound by McNaughton & Gunn
The paper in this book meets the guidelines for
permanence and durability of the Committee on
Production Guidelines for Book Longevity of the
Council on Library Resources.

Printed in the United States of America

04   03   02   01   00   P   5   4   3   2   1

Library of Congress Cataloging-in-Publication Data
Sacks, Peter M.
O wheel : poems / by Peter Sacks.
p.   cm.
ISBN 0-8203-2184-2 (alk. paper)
1. Title.

PS3569.A235 O3 2000
811'.54 21—dc21   99-040055

British Library Cataloging-in-Publication Data available

Poems in this volume first appeared in the following publications: *The Boston Review, Colorado Review, Conjunctions, The New Bread Loaf Anthology of Contemporary American Poetry, Denver Quarterly, The New Republic, The Progressive, Seneca Review, The Threepenny Review.*

As for the wheels, it was cried unto
them in my hearing, O wheel.

EZEKIEL 10:13

*Grateful thanks
to the Guggenheim Foundation
for a grant that enabled me to complete this book.*

CONTENTS

I

THE TREE

This was a different sound, repeated from the other side pressed to the dis-
   appearing throat,
face, fingers, memory of.

The door blew wide on swells that shone back through the tree the ocean
   swung from—
single leaf.

Branch by branch you climbed to where the voices rained.

You held up the song, frayed to the whispered friction of grass when wind
   drops & the
meadow whistles under a dipping finch

the surf swept backward by a larger breath than you could draw till now.

Releasing everything, you climbed again among the others reaching through

to where the world, surprised by hearing pieces of its name, looks back
   into the crowd of
those still vanishing. Who called?

OFFERING

Intolerable

hands
untwisted only

to new
instruments

of sound
over the earth's

own mortar-
pitted

brand caught
fleeing out of

chaos
funneled grit &

bonesmoke

climbing
north over the

cropped &
varnished
heads

night watch night
wall dug

through each new
descendent

filing
the unfinished

iron chamber
music

sharpening.

CALLING

Woken by
the always less than

full-strength
angel

fists clenched
mouth still open

undergone

you had to look around

——

I swallowed I began to
swallow river-bank

stone root stump
graft of who lay back?

whose plough?

——

To separate the words: black furrow

ox axe spine
inconstant constant

gold streaks straggling fortune
sweet juice in your mouth
for what?—

just there
below the shag of

—

doublings where the blade

shears through each
further version

—

death each way

—

white scales
the high unsentencing

—

set free (his representing
power of another kind)

—

before the end
I cut the whole wings

from my heart.

THE TRIAL

Dark flame seeding
rimless

bolted

will & matter
indistinguishable

until they had
invented God

one God.

———

I felt it
in the warning

downward

leaf & branch
beneath

their fingers
rapid

murderous
(& there was music

—hacking)

(cities multiplied)

the defile
late cut deep into

the bone
abraded hand-

sewn through
surrendered

needle-grained

the wick &
spending

between worlds.

White boulders,
dry sea bed.

Absolved.

Or is it taken back

under the smoke?

ASK ME

Unlit
channel leaf

I cannot
whistles

everywhere against
the setting

hung to bleed

a thorn-like bow
string blur

sinks into
the throat

define it
red drop

feather

merchandise
unveiled

the flesh
once only

to be sold

this near edge
nothing mercy

flung all
face-of-hearing

lean stone
membrane

dug
who listen

swiftly kept
alongside

lifted
hope how it

would cling
against

necessity

it clings you
do as from

the cliff high
branches and

you will.

FACE

And yet there was
a face on
which the spirit

moved—one
breath drawn
out all-branching &

another following
depths—lit

spindles re-
dividing as
the voice cuts

forward through

salt silt the reeds (we
saw them sway-back

in our wake)—cut

pounded sliced
again—black mat of

memory.

II

LEOPARD

6.v.'91

Malmesbury, Moreesburg, Picketberg, pale orange land, far mountains,
   climbing zig-zag
over Pickenierskloof, valley below, past Citrusdal

then on through serried evergreens, into the Cedarberg and down to
Bloch's cabin, a stream under oaks;

acorns on the roof, paraffin lamp,

first stars flowing from the brim,

dusk, doves, and the treble rattle of frogs, shallows of a deeper peace,

a kind of wheezing, running dry, yet it flows.

There is a further action. Offstage. Out of harmony.

The candle lifts its fingernail of flame.

7.v.'91

Cleared stones, gathered them beneath a single tree, as if the stones were
     fallen fruit.

(Near the hospice off Mains Ave., Kenilworth. Autumn ivy.
Ontario, the house name on a gate.

I'd stopped to write it down.)

Over the mountains red clouds close the valley, bar out day. All ghosts,
     Janine at an iron
farmgate last August, bobbing for a tip. Greta in wildlilies.

8.v.'91

Stone track, frayed edge of a bell.
Through oaks—leaf edge.

Bell of my childhood home, its rotted thong.

Myself made thin—cigar in the Devil's mouth.

My breath once burned around the charred net of these words.

Two mountains parting, joined with each crook of the path—

the profile of two horses; necks.

8.v.'91

At Muizenberg, the racing stallion wet in sunlight. Swinging muscle gloss.
     Foam of the
ocean and its own.

8.v.'91

Downstream between the image of unfallen leaves and those submerged,
    an oakleaf's
dragged by some unseen revolving rim.

Sea of stone, heatwave thickening the lens;
proteas, everlastings, the arrested swell and spray.

Walking up toward Die Rif—in crosslight—
passages of rock glow.

Nothing swings back safe into the tree.

*

A tide of colder air pressed through us, pressing. And the place itself in us.
Unreadable, impervious.

Litter of acorns and last winter's leaves.
Near hill, sunlight growing downward, laying bare—

9/10.v.'91

Four toepads; leopard; tracks beneath my feet; each paw's soft exclamation
    in the dirt—
twilight's animal around me, tawny, of the threshold, stalking, fur of
    daylight and the dark
rosettes.

Mouth open, taste and smell, the dense fermented musk, close by,
my face-mask loosening.

Mandelstam near my right ear; a hard lump in the skull.

Scorpio's tail dipping back into the Milky Way; Sirius stretching his long
　　neck; the
Southern Cross, its dim spare star and Bushman's sack of unlit space; Orion
　　falling back into the oaks.

9.v.'91

Open birdwing, struck match on the rock,

slipping back around the next bend of the pass—

(to step outside: how clear is it?)

warped and fretted stacks eroded
into isolation,

between two bands of stone another mess of generations
slaughter,

bees hover, bees gathering sweetness from hovering, open world.

Rift places where the stone will ring out underfoot,

cedar, cypress, stripped dry
yet rooted by the path,

hollow tone of my own solitude, grinding to a sharper shelving, struck,

then startled bark of a baboon uphill, disappearing into half-burned
　　cedargrove;

my shadow joining shade between two storm-shattered oaks;

shy klipspringers, white rumps;
stone untwitching to a pair of them released,

wild white thistle shimmering across the slopes,

Herrick: *I sing of times trans-shifting*

outcrops knobbed—baboons along the downhill path to Welbedacht,
stepping over a continuous broken lintel.

9.v.'91

Downhill fires powder the crags,
dove calls muddled with falling riverwater,

owl calls, drip and trickle of frogcalls near the running sloot.

*

The poplars lost their gold. I stood up in the pool to watch them blow.

*

As I walked back I thought, *we've parted,* you and I.

*

My only metaphor for dying, more life.

Bright head, shoulder, wing; the day star setting back into the dawn, out
    of the rising spine
the snake the flower.

The actual oaks: greengold, tree of shade within the tree, lumped light.

10.v.'91

Buck barks and the echo joins the silence, so that I thought
    our words, cries, too, remain,
the rind of space;

pool where I was born, reed-fringed,

stone shell now widened and unsealed, boulders, dead growth,
hammerfist of light against the rocks.

10.v.'91

The long grass, random-brilliant.

Have set my father down—pain in the shoulders—
running water poplars soil.

All from the breath this morning, no part of me that wasn't lit,
the wet rock,

reed stems, redder at the base—
great flowing snake of spine

O. M. murmurs *autumn black earth buried leaves;*
says *Rome stone apple rolled away.*

10.v.'91

Webs in the grass, a little welling up of gnats,
of *foison,* fly, the water scribbles, saying what I want to say:

Soften my heart. Then harden it to keep what's here.

(Emerald sunbird on the leafless oak.)

His spine glows lozenges of coal.

11.v.'91

Walking toward me, face the color of tobacco, tea:

meneer is lus vir die loop;
mister loves to walk;
die beste gesels is by die hut, daar sit *ons;*
the best conversation's near the hut, there we *sit;*
bobbejaan krap die eintjies, kanolletjies;
baboons dig up the little onions, bulbs;
seweoefontein, tafelberg, tweeberge, uitsgatnaaldeberg;
die dieptrek;
ja-nee, dis nog droog, die reentjie bly weg
seven-eyes-fountain, table-mountain, two mountains, outer-hole-
    needles-mountain; the jeep-track;
yes-no, it's still dry, the little rain stays away.

11.v.'91

Nothing of myself except heaped over meaning,

a breeze, an overhang of orange rock. The tape is being erased.

11.v.'91

Enlarged, roaming, the unseen leopard. Smoke-like.

Of both worlds.

Languid, ruinous. Accelerating. Held only as *held outward, issuing . . .*

Lyric, ghost-offering of life, lustered mineral of twilight.

Leopard skin. Flesh of resurrection. Pelt. Lyric pelt.

As chosen words *do* carry the shaped residue.

Recharged. Emergent. The rancid odor again.

Scanning boulder caves and ledges. Lurk and freedom. Scanning shadow-play.

Hair prickling. My face pulled off.

12.v.'91

Clouds the shape of mountains.

Water, birdcalls link

through sweet

joy I can't tell from solitude.

Whole valley, sunlit, opening behind me, cloaked.

*

Jogging back, cool air across my neck, a wide
S through scorched sugarbush.

Downrunning water quickened birdcries.

Valley graveplot: lapsing: Du Toit, Van Wyk, *Hier Rus . . . Ons Herder*

Starlight from the hills; coals mantling.

The log breaks open to its glowing book.

12/13.v.'91

"But also the fathers lying in our depths / like fallen mountains; also
dried-up riverbeds / of ancient mothers; also the whole / soundless
landscape under the clouded or clear sky."—Rilke

*

Quick weave; embers; extinction.

*

The speed of what leaves?

*

Seen from below. Riding the riverlight.

*

Ruin and promise.

The one inhuman solitary pressure of the spirit's love. Bound.

13.v.'91
Broken wheel.

Nothing outside—nothing that is not my track.

Birds flushed shuddering from the grass.

Passion where the shock hits current.

And brings the image. And the image riding it.

13.v.'91
Climbing fast down lower buttresses, last light torches on the riverwater,
    upward
through long grass, then shingled sand; then the half-light lifts.

*

Knowing now how daylight leaves this valley, how the shadows
    drop downslope
over fynbos, few oaks, grove of poplars, how it leaves only the far banded
    slow peak in the
east, then chalk, then ash.

III

SPUR

There'd been
the sound of

cantering.

Through wire I
saw

you look back

out of the quarry
shadows sunk

past sequencing

my other
lives

long-fanged—

our last
words hardening

the only road.

REFUGE

Circling mountain cities
of another

country—

thin wolf
running

with the snow

between
my teeth—I

offered
the fluorescent

nurse black
tracks of

linen long
enough

to wrap your charred

hands back into
oblivion—

the bolt

unleashed

a rifle barrel pointing
out

late harvest
carcasses

the wagon-
rutted

borders

look
the sack of

my despair
thrown

to the gravel—

this was freedom

choking under
frozen waters

gnawing at
the blind face

of the shore.

THE CHANGE

Appearance
clings to

being

my defense

light steps
braided

animal

above the ridge

endured

my doing as
his tongue

required

said *thorn*

hedge flickers

will remain

I rushed gray

terraces

unshielded the

scatter-shot

majority

hauled off
& swung

*let it come
down*

our second
shoreline

heaped
hazing into

bush the late

regime

robed in
the chambers

sworn.

CHOICE

Door to door
the drag-

search
shot through

caution

our unshackled

marrow-fleck
& mineral

finding more than

offshoots

blood spun

rapid-thickened

battering the

singular

inhuman

as charged—

do you think
I did not

wish to take
your hands

that
narrative

not grief flung

swallowed
fully

as the future
comes out of its

hiding stem
seed-coma

famished

for the form
of its own

perishing within
us

pull me now
from inside

further
into you

remorseless—

& we give it
life.

CHARTER

I

Surround-
sound
they unwind

the bandage
push light—
you could

plough
welts you
could plough

through
the sound
unbalancing

dust
no savior
handing

splinters of
another country—
staggering the

torso-work
the carrying the
corpse—

go back and
look ahead start
with the city

pumping
itself dry
into the street.

II

But I was
in the cage

you spoke a backlit

wedge fed
deep into the

pulse-wall
needling

smoke—
Don't leave

(between
the bars)

Don't stop—

You kept your
word—

unrescued

cutting in.

UNTITLED

Given the biblical mirrors stripping
daylight through a mound of the no longer visible

we said it was a murderous intention come to pass.

Knee-deep. With hooded lanterns. Wading in.

———

Remembering the claim, another
split log crammed into the clock

of marrow-bones.
Old leather

gnawed through the hill.

———

Thus far afraid to shut my eyes
the features of the face stand forth.

Had there been grounds for hope

had there been other grounds?

The man has moved.
A navigable smell of blood-rot.

Shaking off the flies.

REACH

The true
peace-

keeping force
your point of hearing

chained through

each horizon

out of scarcity
four-handed

sounds
two ears—we said—

spent shells

already
waiting veins cut

lengthwise where
the furrow

soars
back overhead

unkindling

will not come down.

LOOK IN YOUR HEART

Unshelled

floatrock and mother-lode.

The mountain sagged then broke apart,

each ounce so concentrated nothing held
whatever stamp of its disfiguring

the mind made uncontainable.

Gloved tongues.

The body wrapped and set where space had been.

Crush out the breath crush out the words
they feed and carry it away.

Where we have fallen.

Crawling out.

IV

TWO MOUNTAINS 1

29.v.'90   *Utah*

A giant finger slips through, the planet jewel flashing into space;

my father's hand, the planet cracked, delivering, his hand wrist arm wide
    shoulders,
chest unshadowed, bracing gravity, until he cannot

put it down—the cities folding on themselves more bodies crammed—can
    show me
nothing else—stooped now, & shrinking, shivering—blanket around him

of the dawn,

my own blue arms outspread each side of the escarpment, empty, looking out—

then from behind, pressed to my neck
the sharp blade

(in front, downsloping terraces,
forget-me-nots, wild flax)

sing out, the blade says,
sing.

10.viii.'90   *Cape Town*

Our first approach breaks off against the gale—veers wide,
woodsmoke over townships, camps, a further spread of cardboard,
corrugated iron, the bush scraped clear along False Bay—high
whitecaps—scrolled—

the tail of a caught fish slamming chestwall throat.

10.viii.'90

Shrunken, blade, all but unfleshed skull
through which eyes—

(tracksuit top & pants, green raincoat, scarf, hat, gloves)—shone

shuffling toward me, stick in one hand, *Hello Boy,*

birdboned, wrapped, more like a burn victim,
the bright look steadying,

my turning to the luggage—hypnotic circling—side by side—

a cross-wind from the sea, his free hand on my arm.

11.viii.'90

Instead of holding up the book & silver cup, he leaves them on the
table, hands down against the cloth. I've never seen him lose his
place till now. Too weak to break the bread, *You do it,* lips thin across
his teeth, wind still heaving at the door.

From the tub lift him; stranded body; lift the sunken, the hanging.
Only the voice emphatic, though a little higher, husked, *Thanks boy,*
just bring the towel. Dry him. Saw him once grip a heavy beach-towel
by each end & rub it fast across his chest, down the whole front,
relish, irresistible, cape-like across the back.

13.viii.'90   *Muizenberg*

Unveiling Ouma's tomb, beach sand, hedges of Port Jackson willows,
MOLLY SACKS.

Turned back to watch him,

the wind snatching his hat.

Danny Ipp still mourning Greta further off among the graves.

14.viii.'90

High palms at Heathfield, flowering gums along Boyes Drive, white
butterflies kindling, wind-led, wind-distracted vagrancy; new moon past
Constantia Nek, evening star,

tip of the snail's horn,

the whole night now one corrugation in the bark of an enormous palm,
slow self-balanced creak of fronds.

Sponge & lustral water in the bucket.

12.iv.'90   *Los Angeles*

(When did the sound begin?) the trace of iodine crawling salt stone
dragged across the unhatched scattering of shocks the shell pushed
to no future anchorage now pitching past this shadow-breath cast
through near voices mouthing *tell us what you know* the harrow
heaving under city street land tree bird listening as the afterwave
beats up into the mumbling rocked uncoiling toward you coming
after but for whom the lit grain of the wave now driven to the rock
ledge cries repeated not passed through the thickened grate & slurry
as they build the wash thrown forward . . .

15.viii.'90   *Cape Town*

Hangklip: drunk fisherman between Kalk Bay harbor & the Liquor Den—
shad, salmon, kabeljou—he grips the fish under the gills

& holds them out to passing cars.

He drinks the fish.

16.viii.'90

Here, take this instead.

Behind shut eyes, crosshatched & sagging, hooded, hesitant.

When were we sewn into this folding & unfolding?

The bull has charged out of the ocean field.

We set the flag against the offshore wind.

Even the wind divides around us.

For a while I keep pace with the dying, then fall behind.

19.viii.'90

Left leg three times larger than the right. Lift his springbok-slippered foot
    into the car,
drive to the hospital.

Heparin drip. Both arms bruised trying to find a vein.

Crabs keep crawling to the house—out of the vlei, between the reeds,
    over the lawn—
one upstairs—staring, crouching, back-leg gone.

Gray winter wind across the Cape,
a gray bird, mute, sits on the wire,

hunched digit.

21.viii.'90

What's verified? What pulls its surplus over death?
A cloth of further visibility,

lining turned out—
waterhole where time & space come down to drink?

The under-sense by which I watch them coming down,

war, history
men back to a home only their injury makes credible.

In gravity. The chariot glistening.

14.iv.'91   In flight. L.A. Cape Town

Was. Means.

"On these two words the accusation rests: 'He *was*, therefore it *means*.'
What if it does not *mean*? Even though he *was*?"

Dry muscle of the heart. A space through which the Kaddish swung back
   to the rusted
hump of praise—

six miles over Greenland—sun behind us—shadows sloping eastward on
   the floes

who may ascend the mountain of the Lord?

or stand within the shadow of His wings?

—the burial pamphlet (kept from Archie's funeral)

slipped into my copy of the *Brothers K*

do not be comforted, but weep,

although Zosimov, dying, tells Alyosha

This is what we were created for:
                              happiness.

14/15.iv.'91

Above the small pool of the reading light,

a mountain pass, a Kurdish refugee hunched double in freezing mud,
   the body of his
daughter in his arms—a lagging voice interpreting, *where can I bury her?*

His sobbing untranslated as he turns away.

Outside Pretoria, a line of mouths, wide-open, crowds with sticks, spears,
   dustpan lids, &
further back, above an armored car, a squared-off visor shielding a stare.

Sockets. Filling. Emptying.

15.iv.1991

His little belt here, but him gone, never to see him, hear him (covering
   eyes with hands).

Do not be comforted.

This, said the elder, is Rachel of old weeping for her children. She will
   not be comforted.
Because they are not.

And I will remember your child in my prayers for the repose of the dead.
What was his name?

Alexei, dear father.

A lovely name.

Ephraim: Is he a pleasant child?

Jeremiah: *Set thee up waymarks. Turn again to these thy cities.*

Do not be comforted.

15.iv.'91   Cape Town

Was means.

Window-shade cracked open—sea at dawn—

fish-eagle, lion, ocean-bull, another continent emerging, bare-back
flood & blockage of the gift.

The sound of what remains.

The self laid open. Net cast further.

High over cloud: the turning sword, the angel, naked; bright narcissus flaring
    at his groin.

15.iv.'91

Listening to David's song of God, God leans down to the psalm on the
    wires, & by
degrees. Crouches.

When he waits he is the eagle. When he leaps, the breaking wave.

16.iv.'91   Cape Town

Birthday lunch, too weak to stand. Help him upstairs, trembling.

Legs a mass of open sores, skin flaps.

The Blue Route Shopping Center. My throat closes as I try to eat.

City of bone.

Scapular erosions, growths into the vertebrae.

Red antenna lights over Constantiaberg.

The speed of song accelerates but not to prayer.

A bright bird perches on a dead tree in the vlei.

Unsheathed.

The world revolving in the prowess of the world.

17.iv.'91
Doctor Roy, *Hoe gaan 'it, alles onder beheer?* (Everything under control?)

Pills in the eyewash glass: *nie te sleg nie, met jou?* (Not too bad, with you?)

Sheet drawn to keep flies off.

18.iv.'91
Awake. Between the last & first trains.

18.iv.'91
Two mountains.

18.iv.'91

You say *it's written* (won't increase the morphine).

Moments. Nowhere.

Write now what comes to mind.

What comes to mind now in the sand.

The word *so*.

Sand in the grate.

14.v.'91   *Cape Town*

Pre-dawn. Raid in Swanieville, Inkatha hostel-dwellers rampage through
the shantytown.
27 dead; charred corpse in the street, right arm raised.

The woman screaming by her husband. Will not leave until the corpse has
been removed.
The boy with a bike-spoke through his neck.

Where else kill what you cannot stand?

Wild speeding up of change to absolute.

What altar? What sacrifice? No smoke ascends.

The walls *take in* the smoke.

14.v.'91

Abel knows what Cain knows.

I know two kinds of certainty—

Do not give me the margin to feel beyond circumstance.

Abel knows what Cain knows.

The stone will strip whatever keeps us from life.

15.v.'91

Must form itself become the work of anguish?

Alive & dead at once,

I know two kinds of certainty. Not how to join them.

15.v.'91

And then his smile.

Flayed by Apollo. Departing breath winds through the instrument.

Per letiziar lassu folgor s'acquista / si come riso qui.

Now sleeping.

(By joy up there brightness is won.)

Clink of a teaspoon in a glass.

They call the hoist a monkeychain—a short trapeze hung from its hook.
He clings.

(Penitence. The graduated climb.)

The moment swells above us, breaks.

A dead moth rocks on the linoleum.

17.v.'91

Prior; subsequent; from under.

Things, the wooden hull, its number visible by day, sbh97bn, the orange
    thwarts, the
rope that disappears.

Names, images. Our outcasting.

Or the interval between this space (laid open, pressed) & the emerging
    words—haunting,
maculate, unhidden, doubling back

(so that I often turned to go)

as a moving body casts a shadow and the shadow moves more swiftly as
    it lengthens,

so the issuance accelerates, enlarging—

"in the ultraviolet regions in which chemical changes are produced,"

invent a credible sacrifice,

communal,

true to pain as joy.

Invent a credible sacrifice.

TWO MOUNTAINS 4

20.v.'91   Umfolozi, Natal

On foot through hip-high grasses to the river bank.

Fifty yards upwind, black-maned. The lion's peaceful tearing, chewing,
slowing everything, as if one heavy paw lay on the wheel.

Looking for the first time at a still colonial map of Africa, was told we
    lived at the foot.

Unremovable sensation of the continent pressed down on us.

The lion rips another chunk.

Back off; cross the river, shoes in hand, watching for crocodiles.

Suspend even the action of suspending—mud-slip, running-water underfoot—

& now the phrase, as if not heard before, repeated in the inner
    ear, *city of man*—

more lion-tracks on the other bank, my bare feet fitting widthwise in
    the outline of
the pads. The prints left there.

22.v.'91   *Umhlali*

Each time along this shore-line coming back across what seam?

Two birds too quick to be identified wince by & swerve behind the
leaves of wild banana trees, long creepers, leaf-rot in the
undergrowth decaying to the earth's own backwash, sedimented
rootsmell, brackish clay resurfacing, a living carcass turning inside
out, flesh of the opened face no human face contains.

The massive tongue.

No outside to the labyrinth.

23.v.'91

Phone calls from Cape Town. Still won't increase the morphine. It's
the first time they have talked together openly about the dying.
Should we leave the country or keep waiting?

Near faces, objects in the room, chair, photos, rug, sheet, give of
     the pillow at his head.

Paralyzed below the waist, skin tissuing. How do we hold him?

Crouching for cover. Mute.
Treading water. Stunned under the hull.

To fling myself out like a chunk of bait.
A rabbi screaming insults at the congregation.

Turmoil of the sea at night. A self-wasting. An ungovernable trace.

23/24.v.'91

The figure says "It is to stop his limbs from weeping"—burnishing
his arms & legs with shoe-polish, a thick crust hardening every inch
of skin. "It's death," I shout, "you're casing him in it!" Turns, hits
me hard—a shovel blow—starts severing now until his last nerve-
centers have been snipped away.

And after this she comes back everywhere.

24.v.'91

Look back city: flicker your world of parts.

The townships smoke.

Knobkerrie in one hand, the old man tells of bush-buck he once hunted
   here, gone now.
Under crust.

Blunt wedge of light under the door.

30.v.'91   Cape Town

He lifts his head as I walk in, clasps me whispering "fantastic
fantastic," sees Barbara entering "yes, little rat?"—rain rumpling
the windows, slanting in between the mountain & vlei—drifts back
twitching, eyes roll backwards, hands fret everything around him,
reaching for hallucinated threads, his fingers tying small knots in
the body of the air, searching, pushing his pajama sleeves back,
muttering labor wards & anesthetics, asking if a patient were in
pain, asking mother does she have her horse, something about the
stove, did they get the answer, if so well & good, if not not, does the
oven light come on?

Throughout, his sweetness, boyish, swimming back to focus,
bringing me back stunned—pupils tiny, & the hand trying to
approach his face, slow, faintest touch, a scratching motion, "every
little piece," he says, "under the microscope," the rain close in, I
saying it was fine, smoothing the bed,

to Roy, "No light in this tunnel, boy," the whole body blind.

2.vi.'91

Coots on the vlei with their young, nest in the reeds.

Green V of the pajama, shiny plate of skin over the bone.

All hardening, or changing scale?

Blank intervals when sorrow lets us drop only to change its grip.

12.vi.'91

The smell here at the verge of breath, bone;

raveled flower of the sea, the study of

its motion—breach to glide, the wheel's dolphin-muscled rim turns over
   vaulting—

carried by it, fraying to some further membrane—near light deepened
   through unpeeling
waves.

And what is *not* this membrane, not this other

mind? The cave;

the shadow of the blue boat rocking on gray waters, smoke of violets
    in the gate;

blank dazzlement in the white eye;

mashed fabric of erasures; gloss on nothingness;

the desert folded back.

21.vi.'91   L.A./Jo'burg.

Arrive Jo'burg, Syd there, tells me he's died; phone mother,

will I speak (no rabbi), funeral this afternoon.

21.vi.'91   Cape Town

Landing in a hard wind, winter light against the mountain—bright, dead.

Mother at the house. Against the wall the mirrors draped.

Stand here, sit there, draw breath, walk, speak, & now, again, draw breath,
    draw breath.
Unwanted food.

Danny brings a tie & a razor for the *treuer* cut; reminds me two steps
back then forward for *osei shalom* before the end of Kaddish, drives us to
the cemetery, people waiting, cars parked in among the willows . . . met
by the two *chavrei kidasha* (came at 11:30 Wednesday, sat with the body
through two nights, prepared it) coffin in the hall, we ushered to a side
room as people enter . . .

I say I want to see him, they say no, they'd have to clear the hall, I
say do it, for one minute, go up, fold back a velvet coverlet, the coffin,
open it, a kind of tissue as if gift-wrap, then two cloths over the face,
untreated, shrunken, yellowed, tightened upward, lips apart, teeth
showing, chin now smaller, eyes shut, eyebrows only part unchanged.
I ask can I kiss him, no, forbidden, rewrap, close.

Cantor singing, *all his ways are judgment: who can say*

to the angel, stay thy hand?

I speak.

The fallen reins, admonishment.

The portion of "no God?"

Cantor's mouth, my left hand, mother weeping quietly.

The double-doors blow open at the back, she murmurs no, don't close them,

bright space, "as the flower of the field,"

"it is not thy duty to complete the work, but neither art thou free to
   desist from it,"

then from the hall the coffin lifted, wheeled; open grave; beach sand, three
   shovels upright
in the mound, trench, two planks across it,

then lowered by straps, & I begin the shoveling, one handful then
   two spadefuls on
the lid,

rasp of spade, earthbeat, first explosions, then sand on sand,

mauve stormclouds shut the mountains,

wash hands at brass tap near back door of the hall.

21/22.vi.'91
Sleepless in a strobe behind shut lids. Sail, planet, in the offing.

Sail, tongue, flay open. Show me wings, reins, fountain, mesh hauled,
bright knife rasping at the open center, licked through, evil sucked &
swallowed, throat still opening back past scarcity & greed toward a
formless clarity too dense to enter. Show me.

22/23.vi.'91

Awake again from midnight to near-dawn.

The cantor facing straight into the wall. The candle in its cloudy
    glass. The old men
murmuring—

lid up now & the rain through, rotting, my own face collapsing
    inward, eyes
through cavities, a thin gray paste that drains & disappears.

Boom & shockwave at the edge of spoken words.

24.vi.'91

His shoes, sweaters, neckties from UCT, Natal Carbineers, the Royal
    College, mother
buttoning, labeling cartons, Operation Hunger, Highlands House.

25.vi.'91

Rain ends. Walk the mountain, bending to the mountain water,
washing, drinking; write it down—

peeled bark of bluegums; fynbos; climbing wildgrass, dark green finely
tufted, near-papyral; proteas; leucospermum, glabrum (orange) or
reflexum (yellow); sunbird drinking through its long curved beak, works
whole wheel of the flower; marshrose (*skaamblom)* hangs its head—

into the flesh of numbness, page—of punishment.

26.vi.'91

Cards & letters cover the empty bed.

Jupiter & Venus on one string, Mars between.

29.vi.'91

Path still damp, small white oxalis dotted everywhere on herb-like stems,
    star-scatter in the
Milky Way. Where was I traveling?

3.vii.'91   *Massachusetts.*

The uncut grasses, barley-colored.

Dream of paralysis, unable to call out. Brain washed away. Slurred dirt.
As if one asked a piece of earth to move.

4.vii.'91

Birdcalls, fragmentary, hovering.

Images of him, dressed in rags of his own blood.

Reiterations mingled with the insects; creak & whisper of the field.

The blue sky opening around its stem of fire.

10.vii.'91

Of power. Under history. Unmantled. Pressing up.

13.vii.'91

Thread by thread the net set wide to lift & hold.

14.vii.'91

Mound of underglints, halo & threshing floor.

V

STORY

A lit scratch comes and goes.
Compared to, tearing to compare.

The strongman wrapped in chains.

Unfed, still huge.

Shaking the dust of music from her feet
she comes according to an argument

outlasting everything—starlight between new leaves,

dark berries in her mouth, juice on
the muscles of his arm, his chest,

iron links against her teeth.

(Then we were out.)

(Then we were out for blood.)

THE OCEAN, NAMING IT

Less than a mile out I was
exhausted.

Ghosting out of history;

it came again,
betrayal, so called,

spear-head.

And its eye
stared.

*

Excuses
horned around me, crescent, manifold.

*

Asleep on the dunes.

The moon came up so large I rolled aside.

Involuntary whiteness of the crests

spilled flashing for each generation.

Early stars hung low over the wake.

The future comes toward us.

Every word.

*

Travelling in the cage.

Not fully formed.
                    And there were
many cages.

VOTIVE

The wind's offshore.
It hollows out each swell,
rips spray—back-hanging, gone.

Forget the rivers and the native land,
the dream of justice, even between
three or two, swept clear.

This crowded
still it gives back memory, the sea.

And love too steadies the gaze.

"As for what lasts, the poet sets it down."

*

The bullet, scarfed under the current,
fleshed, alive, rind-red.

No one would keep us.

*

Branched-through, everywhere unwritten
black stem earthed in.

Your want willed,

reknotted: time.

*

The underhang picked bare.

Faster.

Where the tracks had been.

*

It finds us out, sees further (sifting),
cut against the swell of

sapphire. Side by side.

*

So bodied, blameless—blamed.

What were we waiting for?

*

The slope called back out of the root-surge.

Undergone, I knew you.

From the single keel.

*

I knew you.

73

ELECTION

Where
we've come to
by no other way

——

the red stone sleeps
from hand to hand

——

look up
that unflawed

——

steadiness—

——

your hive of
signals
entering—

——

the other wheels
dream a little

wing-work,
levers, cogs,

transparent leaps
& bridges

netted up
across the

purpose
bending now

——

the good

——

thought weighing in,
the structure under it

——

a different

power

——

good (as on 13.i.'98)
devoted to it—

——

kindness

——

then you know
it will be longer—

——

to be wrought

——

O western
fear

——

new votes
the long lines

counted

——

through
(as in we're through)

——

afraid of
my own actions

——

doubled
(dusk)

——

pursuing,

laying hold.

CHANNEL

12.i.'98

Unrutted

13.i.'98

traces widening

14.i.'98

through whose new

15.i.'98

never-
catching-up-with-it

unwilled

enlargements
crowded in

i.'98

not breathing,
not with you

i.'98

what is ideal
when loved?

'98

unless

back-oceaned
twisting

———

'98

the indifferent fury

———

over time

———

replacing

blank (verb)

———

new
misery?

———

finds
its level

———

draws out

———

passion

———

nailed,

———

reflogged upward—

———

shows itself.

RELIEF

We never wanted
immortality.

——

Our present business
frays a further

downfall

——

rearranged;

——

wet hands of the governor
pad & knuckle smear

a witness-crowd damp
with

untouchability

——

I asked the slave
to sing

——

sleep after

love

——

the crowbar

bedded in the
well of tears.

——

New money changing

hands.

——

Who vanishes?

——

What did we
want behind

the currency?

——

The entire class
swept

grappling

——

the last reef-
throated

instrument

——

held thrashing

then hung

——

where the bare tree

surges—

——

God-framed

competitive

——

I said I'd never

felt

such happiness

——

enlarged &

touching

lip tongue

slipping
rim of

possibility

———

the night
we moved the whole

relief

ungated

———

into life received

new bodies
pressing

mesh sunk

back into the

———

cresting
recollection

rushing past us
taken in

& parting:

———

Steer

———

Press back

———

Through rain the

legal bits

blocked in

for accuracy reach

———

a rock-
stain in the weave

your face
still at the glass

through streets

that section
slowed-down of

the city—

muscle,
skin.

———

Under the carved
lid.

———

Nearer.

Freely.

———

Waiting to be killed.

FOR THE DEAD

Truth is
hard, the end

sudden,

and justice like
wisdom distant

and generous.

According to

unbroken memory
the elements were

blessed,

beginning with
open waters

earth
already

leavening the
intercession

of each
word the blood

commended

given back—

even this glance
voice touch now

sliding off

against
the blank

high-engined
reaches

carried

eastering
above that

shoreline the
night-branching

tree bends
under us,

last seen
last heard,

the always-
interrupted

gesture leading,

look it is
not narrow

stripped of all
but terror

until that too
tears free—

face to

new face

shocked but
drawn through

tendrils reaching
chest to

shoulder-blades
the ache

& laboring
compelled,

through-lit,

the black throne
with its body

wrung &
chattering—

for we

can
breathe

this dust &
salt-stained

distance from

each other's

eyes hands mouth

in flight
the image of,

full-throated—

gone where

justice
will not turn

back measuring
itself

against each
downward-

lengthened

remnant
of our

ravening.

NOTES

"Leopard." The quotation from Rilke is from the third Duino Elegy, translated by Stephen Mitchell.

"Refuge." This poems draws motifs and phrases from two poems by H. Leivick: "With the holy poem," translated by Robert Friend, and "Sanatorium," translated by Cynthia Ozick.

"Change." The phrase "Appearance clings to being" is from Simone Weil, *Gravity and Grace*, 34.

"For the Dead." The opening italicized lines are from Shmuel HaNagid, an eleventh-century Hebrew poet, translated by Peter Cole.

THE CONTEMPORARY POETRY SERIES

Edited by Paul Zimmer

Dannie Abse, *One-Legged on Ice*
Susan Astor, *Dame*
Gerald Barrax, *An Audience of One*
Tony Connor, *New and Selected Poems*
Franz Douskey, *Rowing Across the Dark*
Lynn Emanuel, *Hotel Fiesta*
John Engels, *Vivaldi in Early Fall*
John Engels, *Weather-Fear: New and Selected Poems, 1958–1982*
Brendan Galvin, *Atlantic Flyway*
Brendan Galvin, *Winter Oysters*
Michael Heffernan, *The Cry of Oliver Hardy*
Michael Heffernan, *To the Wreakers of Havoc*
Conrad Hilberry, *The Moon Seen as a Slice of Pineapple*
X. J. Kennedy, *Cross Ties*
Caroline Knox, *The House Party*
Gary Margolis, *The Day We Still Stand Here*
Michael Pettit, *American Light*
Bin Ramke, *White Monkeys*
J. W. Rivers, *Proud and on My Feet*
Laurie Sheck, *Amaranth*
Myra Sklarew, *The Science of Goodbyes*
Marcia Southwick, *The Night Won't Save Anyone*
Mary Swander, *Succession*
Bruce Weigl, *The Monkey Wars*
Paul Zarzyski, *The Make-Up of Ice*

THE CONTEMPORARY POETRY SERIES

Edited by Bin Ramke

J. T. Barbarese, *New Science*
J. T. Barbarese, *Under the Blue Moon*
Stephanie Brown, *Allegory of the Supermarket*
Scott Cairns, *Figures for the Ghost*
Scott Cairns, *The Translation of Babel*
Richard Chess, *Tekiah*
Richard Cole, *The Glass Children*
Martha Collins, *A History of a Small Life on a Windy Planet*

Martin Corless-Smith, *Of Piscator*
Christopher Davis, *The Patriot*
Juan Delgado, *Green Web*
Wayne Dodd, *Echoes of the Unspoken*
Wayne Dodd, *Sometimes Music Rises*
Joseph Duemer, *Customs*
Candice Favilla, *Cups*
Casey Finch, *Harming Others*
Norman Finkelstein, *Restless Messengers*
Dennis Finnell, *Belovèd Beast*
Karen Fish, *The Cedar Canoe*
Albert Goldbarth, *Heaven and Earth: A Cosmology*
Pamela Gross, *Birds of the Night Sky/Stars of the Field*
Kathleen Halme, *Every Substance Clothed*
Jonathan Holden, *American Gothic*
Paul Hoover, *Viridian*
Austin Hummell, *The Fugitive Kind*
Claudia Keelan, *The Secularist*
Maurice Kilwein Guevara, *Postmortem*
Caroline Knox, *To Newfoundland*
Steve Kronen, *Empirical Evidence*
Patrick Lawler, *A Drowning Man Is Never Tall Enough*
Sydney Lea, *No Sign*
Jeanne Lebow, *The Outlaw James Copeland and the Champion-Belted Empress*
Phillis Levin, *Temples and Fields*
Gary Margolis, *Falling Awake*
Mark McMorris, *The Black Reeds*
Jacqueline Osherow, *Conversations with Survivors*
Jacqueline Osherow, *Looking for Angels in New York*
Tracy Philpot, *Incorrect Distances*
Donald Revell, *The Gaza of Winter*
Martha Ronk, *Desire in L.A.*
Martha Ronk, *Eyetrouble*
Peter Sacks, *O Wheel*
Aleda Shirley, *Chinese Architecture*
Pamela Stewart, *The Red Window*
Susan Stewart, *The Hive*
Terese Svoboda, *All Aberration*
Terese Svoboda, *Mere Mortals*
Lee Upton, *Approximate Darling*
Arthur Vogelsang, *Twentieth Century Women*
Sidney Wade, *Empty Sleeves*
Marjorie Welish, *Casting Sequences*
Susan Wheeler, *Bag 'o' Diamonds*
C. D. Wright, *String Light*
Katayoon Zandvakili, *Deer Table Legs*